VIETNAM
TRAVEL BOOK

*Discover the Hidden Gems of Vietnam:
An Unforgettable Journey through
Culture, Cuisine, and Adventure*

Celicia Hass

Chapter 1: Introduction

It was a warm and sunny day in Hanoi, Vietnam when I arrived, feeling excited and slightly nervous to explore this new and unfamiliar country. As I walked through the crowded streets and narrow alleyways, I was struck by the sights, sounds, and smells of the city: the honking of motorbikes, the aroma of street food, and the colorful displays of goods for sale.

Over the next few weeks, I traveled throughout Vietnam, taking in the diverse landscapes, rich culture, and delicious cuisine. I hiked through the mountains of Sapa, explored the ancient city of Hue, and lounged on the sandy beaches of Nha Trang. I tasted the tangy flavors of Vietnamese pho, the sweet and savory combination of banh mi sandwiches, and the refreshing taste of iced coffee with condensed milk.

But as I traveled, I also encountered challenges and surprises. I struggled to communicate with locals who didn't speak English, haggled with vendors over prices, and got lost navigating the winding streets of Hoi An. At times, I felt frustrated, overwhelmed, and even a bit homesick.

Yet despite the challenges, I fell in love with Vietnam. I was inspired by the resilience and friendliness of the people, the beauty of the natural landscapes, and the vibrant energy of the cities. I felt a deep sense of gratitude for the opportunity to explore a new culture and expand my horizons.

As my trip drew to a close, I found myself reflecting on all that I had learned and experienced. I realized that there was so much more I could share with others who were planning to visit Vietnam. I wanted to create a guide that would help other travelers navigate the nuances of the culture, find the best food and accommodations, and experience the most memorable activities and attractions.

So, I made the decision to author this guide, drawing on my own experiences and research to create a comprehensive resource for others who are planning to visit Vietnam. I poured my heart and soul into the project, excited to share my passion for this amazing country with others.

And now, as I look back on my journey and the guide I created, I feel a deep sense of pride and accomplishment. I know that my guide will help others have a smoother, more enjoyable trip to

Vietnam, just as my own experiences and challenges have enriched my life in countless ways.

About Vietnam

Vietnam is a beautiful and fascinating country located in Southeast Asia, bordered by China to the north, Laos to the northwest, Cambodia to the southwest, and the South China Sea to the east. Vietnam is known for its stunning natural landscapes, rich culture and history, and delicious cuisine, making it a popular travel destination for visitors from around the world.

Vietnam is a country with a long and complex history, including periods of colonization, war, and communism. However, in recent decades, Vietnam has undergone significant economic and social development, with a growing tourism industry, modern cities, and a vibrant culture.

Some of the most popular tourist destinations in Vietnam include the bustling cities of Ho Chi Minh City and Hanoi, the stunning natural landscapes of Ha Long Bay and Sapa, and the historic cities of Hue and Hoi An. Visitors to Vietnam can also enjoy delicious cuisine, including famous dishes like pho, banh mi, and spring rolls, and experience traditional arts and cultural performances.

Whether you're interested in history, culture, cuisine, or nature, Vietnam offers something for everyone. With friendly locals, affordable prices, and a unique blend of tradition and modernity, Vietnam is an unforgettable destination that will leave you with memories to last a lifetime.

Geography and climate

Vietnam is a long and narrow country that stretches over 1,000 miles (1,600 km) from north to south, with a coastline along the South China Sea. The geography of Vietnam is incredibly diverse, including towering mountains, lush jungles, rolling hills, and expansive coastal plains.

In the north of Vietnam, the landscape is dominated by the rugged terrain of the Hoang Lien Son Mountain range, which includes Fansipan, the highest peak in Indochina at 3,143 meters. The region is also home to terraced rice paddies that have been cultivated by ethnic minority groups for centuries.

The northeastern part of Vietnam is known for its karst formations and the famous Ha Long Bay, a UNESCO World Heritage Site that features thousands of limestone islands and islets.

Central Vietnam is characterized by the Truong Son Mountain range, which runs from north to south through the middle of the country. The area is home to many historic and cultural landmarks, including the old imperial city of Hue and the ancient town of Hoi An, both of which are UNESCO World Heritage Sites.

In the south, the landscape is dominated by the Mekong River Delta, which is the rice bowl of the country and home to a complex network of waterways and canals. The region is also home to the bustling cities of Ho Chi Minh City and Can Tho, as well as the beautiful beaches of Nha Trang and Phu Quoc.

Vietnam has a tropical climate with two main seasons, a rainy season and a dry season. The climate is influenced by the country's location in Southeast Asia, its long coastline, and its mountainous terrain. The weather can vary greatly depending on the region and time of year.

In the north of Vietnam, the winter months (December to February) can be cool and damp, with temperatures averaging around 15°C (59°F). The summer months (June to August) are hot and humid, with temperatures averaging around 30°C (86°F) and frequent rain showers. The best time to visit the north is in the spring (March to May) or the autumn (September to November), when the weather is mild and dry.

Central Vietnam has a warm and dry climate with high temperatures throughout the year. The rainy season runs from September to January, with the heaviest rainfall occurring in October and November. The best time to visit the central region is from February to May, when the weather is mild and dry.

In the south of Vietnam, the weather is warm and humid throughout the year, with little variation in temperature. The rainy season runs from May to November, with the heaviest rainfall occurring in June, July, and August. The best time to visit the south is from December to April, when the weather is dry, and temperatures are pleasant.

Vietnam is also prone to natural disasters, including typhoons, floods, and landslides. The typhoon season runs from July to November, with the central and northern regions most affected. Visitors should be aware of the weather conditions and take necessary precautions, such as checking weather reports and avoiding travel during times of extreme weather.

Overall, the geography and climate of Vietnam offer a diverse and beautiful landscape for visitors to explore, with a range of activities and attractions to suit every interest. From the towering mountains of the north to the lush deltas of the south, Vietnam offers a unique and unforgettable travel experience.

History and culture

Vietnam has a rich and complex history that spans over two thousand years, with periods of colonization, war, and communism. The history of Vietnam has played a significant role in shaping its culture, traditions, and values, which are still evident in the country today.

One of the most notable periods in Vietnam's history was the thousand-year period of Chinese domination, which began in 111 BC. During this time, Vietnam adopted many aspects of Chinese culture, including Confucianism, Buddhism, and the Chinese language.

However, Vietnam also developed its own unique culture, which was characterized by a strong sense of national identity and resistance to foreign influence.

In the 19th century, Vietnam was colonized by the French, who introduced Western ideas, technology, and education. French colonization lasted until 1954, when Vietnamese forces, led by Ho Chi Minh, defeated the French in the battle of Dien Bien Phu. This victory marked the beginning of the Vietnam War, which lasted until 1975 and had a significant impact on Vietnam's culture and society.

Today, Vietnam is a socialist republic with a strong sense of national identity and a deep respect for its history and culture. The country has made significant economic and social progress in recent decades, while also preserving its unique traditions and values.

Vietnamese culture is heavily influenced by Confucianism, which emphasizes the importance of family, education, and respect for authority.

Vietnamese society places a strong emphasis on community and family, with a strong sense of obligation to one's parents and ancestors. Family members often live together and work together, with extended families and close-knit communities being the norm.

Vietnamese cuisine is known for its fresh ingredients, bold flavors, and healthy dishes. Some of the most popular Vietnamese dishes include pho, a savory noodle soup; banh mi, a delicious sandwich filled with meat, vegetables, and herbs; and spring rolls, which are light and refreshing.

Traditional Vietnamese arts and culture are also an important part of the country's heritage. Vietnam has a rich tradition of music, dance, and theater, with many performances taking place at festivals and special events. Vietnamese folk music, including the popular genre of hat cheo, is characterized by its lively and upbeat rhythms and is often accompanied by traditional instruments such as the dan bau and the dan tranh.

Vietnam is also home to a number of historic and cultural landmarks, including the Imperial City of Hue, the ancient town of Hoi An, and the Cu Chi Tunnels, which were used by the Viet Cong during the Vietnam War. Visitors to Vietnam can also experience traditional cultural performances, such as water puppetry shows and ca tru singing.

In conclusion, Vietnam's history and culture are a rich and complex tapestry of influences, traditions, and values that have shaped the country and its people over the course of many centuries. From its thousand-year period of Chinese domination to its colonial history and its struggle for independence, Vietnam has a unique and fascinating story to tell. Today, the country is a vibrant and modern nation that continues to embrace its rich cultural heritage, while also forging ahead with economic and social progress.

Entry requirements

Vietnam is a popular tourist destination, attracting millions of visitors from all around the world each year. To enter Vietnam as a tourist, visitors must comply with certain entry requirements and obtain the necessary visas and permits.

Visa Requirements
Most visitors to Vietnam require a visa to enter the country. The type of visa required will depend on the length of the stay and the purpose of the visit. There are several types of visas available for tourists, including a single-entry visa, multiple-entry visa, and e-visa.

Single-entry visas allow visitors to enter Vietnam once and stay for up to 30 days. Multiple-entry visas allow visitors to enter and exit the country multiple times within a set period of time, typically up to 90 days. E-visas are a relatively new type of visa that can be applied for online and are valid for stays of up to 30 days.

Visa applications must be made in advance, and visitors should allow plenty of time for processing. The application process can be completed online, through a Vietnamese embassy or consulate, or through a travel agent. Fees for visas will vary depending on the type of visa and the country of origin.

Passport Requirements
Visitors to Vietnam must also have a valid passport with at least six months' validity remaining from the date of entry. The passport must have at least one blank page for the visa and entry stamp.

Travelers should also be aware that Vietnam requires visitors to have a return or onward ticket and proof of sufficient funds to cover their stay in the country. Visitors may be asked to provide this information at the border when entering Vietnam.

Health Requirements

Vietnam does not require visitors to have any specific vaccinations to enter the country, but some vaccinations may be recommended depending on the traveler's health and itinerary. Visitors are advised to consult with a doctor or travel health clinic before traveling to Vietnam to discuss any necessary vaccinations or health precautions.

In addition, visitors to Vietnam should be aware of the risk of mosquito-borne illnesses, such as dengue fever and malaria, and take appropriate precautions to avoid mosquito bites. This may include wearing long-sleeved clothing, using insect repellent, and sleeping under mosquito nets.

Currency Restrictions

There are also restrictions on the amount of Vietnamese Dong (VND) that can be brought in and out of the country. Visitors are allowed to bring in up to 15 million VND and must declare any amounts exceeding this limit. Visitors can also take up to 5 million VND out of the country, but amounts exceeding this limit must be declared.

Conclusion

In conclusion, visitors to Vietnam should be aware of the entry requirements and regulations in place when entering the country. These include obtaining the necessary visas and permits, complying with passport and customs requirements, and taking appropriate health precautions. It is important to plan ahead and allow plenty of time for processing visa applications and complying with other entry requirements to ensure a smooth and hassle-free trip to Vietnam.

Time zones

Vietnam is located in Southeast Asia and has a single time zone, which is Indochina Time (ICT). ICT is 7 hours ahead of Coordinated Universal Time (UTC+7).

Daylight Saving Time is not observed in Vietnam, so the time zone remains the same throughout the year. This means that if it is 12:00 pm (noon) in Vietnam, it is 5:00 am in Coordinated Universal Time (UTC).

It is worth noting that some parts of Vietnam, particularly in the northern mountainous region, use a different time zone known as Vietnam Time

(VIT), which is one hour behind ICT. However, this time zone is not officially recognized and is only used locally in some areas.

Travelers to Vietnam should adjust their watches and devices to ICT when arriving in the country to avoid any confusion or scheduling issues. It is also a good idea to check the time difference when planning international flights or connecting with people in different time zones.

Chapter 2: Top Destinations in Vietnam

Hanoi

Hanoi is the capital city of Vietnam and a popular tourist destination. The city is known for its rich history, traditional architecture, delicious street food, and vibrant cultural scene. Here's what you need to know when visiting Hanoi as a tourist:

Getting There

Hanoi has an international airport, Noi Bai International Airport (HAN), located about 35 kilometers from the city center. Visitors can fly directly to Hanoi from major cities in Asia, Europe, and Australia. Taxis and ride-hailing services are available at the airport to take you to your accommodation.

Getting Around

Hanoi has a well-connected public transportation system, including buses, trains, and taxis. The city is also relatively compact, making it easy to explore on foot. Visitors can also rent a motorbike or bicycle to get around.

Sights and Activities

Hanoi has plenty to offer in terms of sights and activities. Some of the must-see attractions include:

- Hoan Kiem Lake: A picturesque lake located in the heart of the city, with a scenic walking path and historic landmarks.

- Old Quarter: A charming neighborhood with narrow streets, traditional houses, and a lively street food scene.

- Ho Chi Minh Mausoleum: A monumental marble structure that houses the embalmed body of Vietnam's iconic leader, Ho Chi Minh.

- Temple of Literature: A well-preserved complex of Confucian temples and gardens, which was Vietnam's first national university.

- Hanoi Opera House: A grand, French-colonial building that hosts performances of opera, ballet, and traditional music.

- Street Food Tours: Hanoi is famous for its street food scene, with local delicacies like pho, banh mi, and egg coffee. Joining a street food tour is a great way to explore the city's food culture.

Accommodation

Hanoi has a range of accommodation options to suit different budgets and preferences. Some of the most popular areas to stay in Hanoi include the Old Quarter, Hoan Kiem, and Ba Dinh. Visitors can choose from budget hostels, mid-range hotels, and luxury resorts.

Safety and Etiquette

Hanoi is a relatively safe city, but visitors should take precautions to protect their valuables and be aware of common scams. It is also important to be respectful of local customs and etiquette. Dress modestly when visiting temples or other religious sites, and remove your shoes before entering someone's home or a sacred place.

Conclusion

Hanoi is a fascinating and vibrant city that has something to offer every traveler. Whether you're interested in history, culture, food, or simply soaking up the atmosphere, Hanoi is a great destination to explore. As a tourist, it is important to plan ahead and take necessary precautions to ensure a safe and enjoyable trip.

Ho Chi Minh City (Saigon)

Ho Chi Minh City, formerly known as Saigon, is the largest city in Vietnam and a popular tourist destination. The city is known for its rich history, vibrant street life, bustling markets, and diverse cuisine. Here's what you need to know when visiting Ho Chi Minh City as a tourist:

Getting There

Ho Chi Minh City has an international airport, Tan Son Nhat International Airport (SGN), located about 7 kilometers from the city center. Visitors can fly directly to Ho Chi Minh City from major cities in Asia, Europe, and Australia. Taxis and ride-hailing services are available at the airport to take you to your accommodation.

Getting Around

Ho Chi Minh City has a variety of transportation options for visitors, including taxis, motorbikes, buses, and the metro. The city is large and spread out, so it may be helpful to hire a private car or motorbike for the day to see multiple sites. Visitors should also exercise caution when walking on the streets, as traffic can be chaotic.

Sights and Activities

- Ho Chi Minh City offers plenty of sights and activities for visitors, including:

- War Remnants Museum: A powerful museum that showcases the impact of the Vietnam War on the country and its people.

- Reunification Palace: A historic palace that served as the headquarters of the South Vietnamese government during the Vietnam War.

- Notre-Dame Cathedral Basilica of Saigon: A stunning cathedral that is a popular photo spot and landmark.

- Ben Thanh Market: A bustling market that sells everything from clothing and souvenirs to street food.

- Cu Chi Tunnels: A network of tunnels used by the Viet Cong during the Vietnam War, which can be explored on a guided tour.

- Mekong Delta: A picturesque region outside of Ho Chi Minh City that offers boat rides, floating markets, and rural landscapes.

Accommodation

Ho Chi Minh City has a range of accommodation options to suit different budgets and preferences. Some of the most popular areas to stay in Ho Chi Minh City include District 1, District 3, and Pham Ngu Lao. Visitors can choose from budget hostels, mid-range hotels, and luxury resorts.

Food and Drink

Ho Chi Minh City is famous for its diverse and delicious cuisine, which includes local specialties like pho, banh mi, and com tam. Visitors should also try the city's street food scene, which offers everything from grilled meats to tropical fruits. It is also recommended to try local beer and coffee, as well as refreshing sugarcane juice and coconut water.

Safety and Etiquette

Ho Chi Minh City is a relatively safe city, but visitors should take precautions to protect their valuables and be aware of common scams. It is also important to be respectful of local customs and etiquette. Dress modestly when visiting temples or other religious sites and remove your shoes before entering someone's home or a sacred place.

Conclusion

Ho Chi Minh City is a vibrant and dynamic city that offers a unique blend of history, culture, and cuisine. Whether you're interested in exploring the city's past, indulging in its food scene, or simply soaking up the atmosphere, Ho Chi Minh City is a great destination to explore. As a tourist, it is important to plan ahead and take necessary precautions to ensure a safe and enjoyable trip.

Halong Bay

Halong Bay is a natural wonder and UNESCO World Heritage site located in the Gulf of Tonkin, in the northeastern region of Vietnam. The bay features thousands of limestone islands and islets rising from the emerald waters, creating a breathtaking landscape that attracts millions of tourists each year. Here's what you need to know when visiting Halong Bay as a tourist:

Getting There

Halong Bay is about 170 kilometers from Hanoi, and visitors can travel to the bay by car or bus, which takes approximately 3-4 hours. Alternatively, there are also seaplanes and helicopter services that offer aerial views of the bay.

Sights and Activities

Halong Bay is primarily known for its stunning landscape and natural beauty, which can be experienced through various activities, including:

- Cruising: One of the most popular ways to explore Halong Bay is by taking a cruise. Visitors can choose from day cruises or overnight cruises, which typically include meals and activities like kayaking, swimming, and fishing.

- Cave exploration: Halong Bay is home to several caves, including the popular Sung Sot Cave, which features unique stalactites and stalagmites.

- Island hopping: Visitors can also take a tour of the various islands in Halong Bay, including Cat Ba Island, which offers hiking trails and a national park.

- Floating villages: Halong Bay is also home to several floating villages, where locals live in houseboats and earn a living from fishing and aquaculture.

Accommodation

Halong Bay offers a range of accommodation options for visitors, including luxury cruise ships, mid-range hotels, and budget hostels. Visitors can choose to stay on a cruise ship for the duration of their stay or opt for land-based accommodations on Cat Ba Island.

Food and Drink

Halong Bay is known for its fresh seafood, which can be enjoyed at the various restaurants and eateries in the area. Visitors can try local specialties like grilled squid, fish curry, and seafood hotpot. It is also recommended to try local beer and rice wine.

Weather

The best time to visit Halong Bay is between September and November, when the weather is dry and the skies are clear. The summer months of June to August can be hot and humid, and there is a risk of typhoons and storms from May to September.

Safety and Etiquette

Visitors to Halong Bay should be aware of safety precautions, including wearing a life jacket when participating in water activities and following the safety guidelines provided by cruise operators. It is also important to be respectful of local customs and etiquette, including dress modestly and remove your shoes before entering someone's home or a sacred place.

Conclusion

Halong Bay is a must-visit destination in Vietnam, offering visitors a unique and unforgettable experience in a stunning natural setting. As a tourist, it is important to plan ahead and take necessary precautions to ensure a safe and enjoyable trip. Whether you're cruising through the limestone islands, exploring the caves, or sampling the local cuisine, Halong Bay is a destination that should not be missed.

Hoi An

Hoi An is a picturesque and charming town located in central Vietnam, known for its well-preserved architecture, rich history, and beautiful scenery. Here's what you need to know when visiting Hoi An as a tourist:

Getting There

Hoi An is located about 30 kilometers south of Da Nang and can be reached by car, taxi, or bus. The nearest airport is Da Nang International Airport, which is approximately 30 minutes away by car.

Sights and Activities

Hoi An is primarily known for its historic architecture, including Japanese bridges, ancient temples, and colorful shop houses. Visitors can explore the town's many attractions, including:

- Old Town: The heart of Hoi An is its old town, a UNESCO World Heritage site featuring historic houses, temples, and museums.

- Japanese Covered Bridge: One of Hoi An's most iconic landmarks, the Japanese Covered Bridge was built in the 16th century to connect the Japanese and Chinese communities in Hoi An.

- Temples and Pagodas: Hoi An is home to several historic temples and pagodas, including the Quan Cong Temple, Phuoc Kien Assembly Hall, and Chua Cau Temple.

- Tailor-made clothes: Hoi An is also famous for its tailor-made clothes, with many shops offering custom suits, dresses, and other garments.

- Beaches: Hoi An is located near several beautiful beaches, including An Bang Beach and Cua Dai Beach.

Accommodation

Hoi An offers a range of accommodation options for visitors, including boutique hotels, hostels, and homestays. Many of the hotels and guesthouses in Hoi An are located in the old town, offering easy access to the town's attractions.

Food and Drink

Hoi An is known for its delicious cuisine, which features a blend of Vietnamese, Chinese, and Japanese influences. Visitors can sample local specialties like cao lau (noodles with pork and herbs), banh mi (Vietnamese baguette), and mi quang (noodles with pork, shrimp, and herbs). The town is also known for its coffee culture, with many cozy cafes serving up traditional Vietnamese coffee.

Weather

The best time to visit Hoi An is between February and May, when the weather is mild and dry. The summer months of June to August can be hot and humid, while the winter months of December to January can be cool and rainy.

Safety and Etiquette

Visitors to Hoi An should be aware of safety precautions, including avoiding drinking tap water and being mindful of traffic when crossing the street. It is also important to be respectful of local customs and etiquette, including dressing modestly when visiting temples and removing your shoes before entering someone's home.

Conclusion

Hoi An is a beautiful and charming town that offers visitors a glimpse into Vietnam's rich history and culture. As a tourist, it is important to plan ahead and take necessary precautions to ensure a safe and enjoyable trip. Whether you're exploring the town's ancient architecture, indulging in its delicious cuisine, or simply relaxing on the beach, Hoi An is a destination that should not be missed.

Hue

Hue is a historic city located in central Vietnam, known for its imperial citadel, ancient tombs, and scenic landscapes. Here's what you need to know when visiting Hue as a tourist:

Getting There

Hue can be reached by car, bus, or train from major cities in Vietnam. The nearest airport is Phu Bai International Airport, which is approximately 15 kilometers from the city center.

Sights and Activities

Hue is primarily known for its rich history and culture, and there are plenty of attractions to explore, including:

- Imperial City: The centerpiece of Hue's cultural heritage is the Imperial City, a walled fortress that was once the seat of the Nguyen Dynasty. Visitors can explore the ornate palaces, temples, and gardens that make up this impressive complex.

- Tombs of the Emperors: Hue is home to several impressive royal tombs, including the Tomb of Tu Duc, the Tomb of Khai Dinh, and the Tomb of Minh Mang. These tombs are a testament to the grandeur and sophistication of the Nguyen Dynasty.

- Thien Mu Pagoda: One of the most iconic landmarks in Hue, Thien Mu Pagoda is a seven-story temple that sits on the banks of the Perfume River. Visitors can climb to the top for stunning views of the surrounding area.

- Perfume River: The Perfume River is a scenic waterway that winds through the heart of Hue. Visitors can take a boat ride along the river to enjoy the views and explore the many temples and pagodas that line its banks.

Accommodation

Hue offers a range of accommodation options for visitors, including budget hostels, mid-range hotels, and luxurious resorts. Many of the hotels and guesthouses in Hue are located near the city center, making it easy to explore the town's attractions.

Food and Drink

Hue is known for its delicious cuisine, which features a blend of royal and local flavors. Visitors can sample local specialties like bun bo Hue (spicy beef noodle soup), banh khoai (Hue-style pancakes), and nem lui (lemongrass skewers). Hue is also known for its strong coffee and sweet desserts.

Weather

The best time to visit Hue is between February and May, when the weather is mild and dry. The summer months of June to August can be hot and humid, while the winter months of December to January can be cool and rainy.

Safety and Etiquette

Visitors to Hue should be aware of safety precautions, including avoiding drinking tap water and being mindful of traffic when crossing the street. It is also important to be respectful of local customs and etiquette, including dressing modestly when visiting temples and removing your shoes before entering someone's home.

Conclusion

Hue is a beautiful and historic city that offers visitors a glimpse into Vietnam's royal past. As a tourist, it is important to plan ahead and take necessary precautions to ensure a safe and enjoyable trip. Whether you're exploring the Imperial City, marveling at the ancient tombs, or simply relaxing along the Perfume River, Hue is a destination that should not be missed.

Sapa

Sapa is a picturesque mountain town in the northern region of Vietnam, known for its breathtaking scenery, vibrant culture, and outdoor adventures. Here's what you need to know when visiting Sapa as a tourist:

Getting There

Sapa is located approximately 380 kilometers northwest of Hanoi and can be reached by train or bus. The most popular way to get to Sapa is by overnight train from Hanoi, which takes around 8-9 hours.

Sights and Activities

Sapa is primarily known for its stunning natural beauty, and there are plenty of activities to enjoy, including:
- Trekking: Sapa is a popular destination for trekking, with several scenic trails winding through the surrounding mountains and valleys. Visitors can explore the local hill tribe villages, enjoy the stunning views of the

rice terraces and waterfalls, and experience the local way of life.

- Markets: Sapa is home to several colorful markets, where visitors can find a variety of local handicrafts, textiles, and fresh produce. The most popular markets include Bac Ha Market, Can Cau Market, and Coc Ly Market.

- Fansipan: Fansipan is the highest mountain in Vietnam, standing at 3,143 meters above sea level. Visitors can take a cable car or trek to the summit for stunning views of the surrounding area.

- Hill Tribe Villages: Sapa is home to several ethnic minority groups, including the Hmong, Dao, and Tay. Visitors can experience the local culture and way of life by visiting the traditional hill tribe villages and learning about their customs and traditions.

Accommodation

Sapa offers a range of accommodation options for visitors, including budget hostels, mid-range hotels, and luxurious resorts. Many of the hotels and guesthouses in Sapa are located near the town center, making it easy to explore the local attractions.

Food and Drink

Sapa is known for its unique cuisine, which features a blend of local and French flavors. Visitors can sample local specialties like thang co (a spicy stew made with horse meat), grilled trout, and banh cuon (steamed rice cakes). Sapa is also known for its locally grown tea, which is available at many of the local shops.

Weather

The best time to visit Sapa is between March and May or September and November, when the weather is mild and dry. The summer months of June to August can be hot and rainy, while the winter months of December to February can be cold and foggy.

Safety and Etiquette

Visitors to Sapa should be aware of safety precautions, including being mindful of the steep and slippery terrain when trekking and avoiding drinking tap water. It is also important to be respectful of local customs and etiquette, including dressing modestly when visiting temples and removing your shoes before entering someone's home.

Conclusion

Sapa is a beautiful and unique destination that offers visitors a glimpse into the traditional way of life of the hill tribes in northern Vietnam. As a tourist, it is important to plan ahead and take necessary precautions to ensure a safe and enjoyable trip. Whether you're trekking through the mountains, shopping at the local markets, or simply enjoying the stunning scenery, Sapa is a destination that should not be missed.

Nha Trang

Nha Trang is a coastal city in the Khanh Hoa province of Vietnam, and it's one of the most popular tourist destinations in the country. It is a place where travelers can relax and enjoy the sun, sea, and sand, as well as explore the local culture and attractions. In this section of the guide, we will expound on Nha Trang as a tourist destination and everything a tourist needs to know.

Attractions and Activities
One of the main draws of Nha Trang is its beautiful beaches. The most famous one is Nha Trang Beach, which stretches for six kilometers and is popular for swimming, sunbathing, and watersports. Other popular beaches in the area include Bai Dai Beach, Doc Let Beach, and Hon Chong Beach.

In addition to the beaches, Nha Trang has several other attractions and activities for tourists. These include:

- Vinpearl Land: A popular amusement park that features a water park, aquarium, and various rides and attractions.

- Long Son Pagoda: A beautiful Buddhist temple that's known for its large white Buddha statue.

- Po Nagar Cham Towers: A set of ancient Cham towers that date back to the 7th century.

- Scuba diving and snorkeling: Nha Trang has several scuba diving and snorkeling spots that offer the opportunity to see colorful coral reefs and marine life.

- Mud baths: Mud baths are a popular activity in Nha Trang, and there are several spas and resorts that offer this experience.

Accommodation

Nha Trang has a wide range of accommodation options, from budget hostels to luxury resorts. The most popular areas to stay in are near the beach, where there are many hotels, resorts, and guesthouses. Some of the most popular hotels and resorts in Nha Trang include:

- Sheraton Nha Trang Hotel and Spa

- Amiana Resort Nha Trang

- Vinpearl Resort and Spa Nha Trang Bay

- Mia Resort Nha Trang

Food and Drink

Nha Trang is known for its seafood, and there are many restaurants in the city that serve fresh fish, crabs, prawns, and other local delicacies. Some of the most popular seafood restaurants in Nha Trang include:

- Lanterns Vietnamese Restaurant

- Lac Canh Restaurant

- Sailing Club Nha Trang

Apart from seafood, Nha Trang also has a variety of Vietnamese and international cuisine available at restaurants and food stalls. There are also many bars and clubs in the city that serve drinks and host events.

Getting Around

Nha Trang is a small city, and most of the tourist attractions and hotels are located near the beach. This means that it's easy to get around on foot or by bicycle. Taxis and motorbike taxis are also available for longer distances or if you prefer not to walk or bike. It's important to negotiate prices with taxi and motorbike taxi drivers before getting in to avoid overcharging.

Conclusion

Nha Trang is a beautiful coastal city with a lot to offer tourists. With its beaches, attractions, and activities, it's a great place to relax and have fun. Whether you're looking for a budget-friendly vacation or a luxurious getaway, Nha Trang has something for everyone.

Da Nang

Da Nang is a coastal city in central Vietnam, and it's a popular tourist destination thanks to its beautiful beaches, delicious cuisine, and unique attractions. Whether you're looking for a relaxing beach vacation or an adventurous getaway, Da Nang has something to offer every type of traveler.

Getting to Da Nang

Da Nang is easily accessible by air, with a major international airport located just a few kilometers from the city center. Several major airlines operate direct flights from cities throughout Asia, including Bangkok, Seoul, and Singapore. If you're traveling domestically within Vietnam, you can also take a train or a bus to Da Nang.

Climate

Da Nang has a tropical climate with two main seasons: the dry season from February to August, and the wet season from September to January. The best time to visit Da Nang is during the dry season when temperatures are mild and rainfall is low. The average temperature during this time is around 25-30°C, making it perfect weather for enjoying the beaches.

Attractions

One of the main attractions in Da Nang is its beautiful beaches. Some of the most popular beaches include My Khe Beach, Non-Nuoc Beach, and Lang Co Beach. These beaches are known for their crystal-clear waters and soft, white sand.

Another must-see attraction in Da Nang is the Marble Mountains, which are a cluster of five limestone hills that are named after the five elements: metal, wood, water, fire, and earth. Visitors can explore the caves and pagodas located within the hills, and enjoy panoramic views of the city and the surrounding countryside.

If you're interested in history, you can visit the Museum of Cham Sculpture, which houses a collection of Cham artifacts and sculptures dating back to the 7th century. You can also visit the Da Nang Cathedral, a pink church built in the French Gothic style that was constructed during the early 20th century.

Food

Da Nang is known for its delicious cuisine, which combines the flavors of northern and southern Vietnam. Some of the must-try dishes include banh xeo, a crispy Vietnamese pancake filled with shrimp, pork, and bean sprouts, and mi quang, a spicy noodle dish that's made with turmeric, shrimp, and pork. You can also sample fresh seafood at the many restaurants and street vendors located throughout the city.

Accommodations

Da Nang has a wide range of accommodations to suit every budget, from luxury resorts to budget-friendly hostels. Some of the top-rated hotels in Da Nang include the InterContinental Danang Sun Peninsula Resort, the Furama Resort Danang, and the Hyatt Regency Danang Resort and Spa.

<u>Getting Around</u>

Da Nang is a relatively small city, and most of the main attractions are located within a few kilometers of each other. The easiest way to get around is by taxi or motorbike, both of which are widely available throughout the city. If you're feeling adventurous, you can also rent a bicycle or a motorbike to explore the city on your own.

Overall, Da Nang is a great destination for travelers looking to experience the beauty and culture of central Vietnam. With its stunning beaches, unique attractions, and delicious cuisine, it's no wonder why it's become such a popular tourist destination in recent years.

Phu Quoc

Phu Quoc is a beautiful island located in the Gulf of Thailand, off the southern coast of Vietnam. The island is known for its stunning beaches, crystal-clear waters, and lush tropical forests. It's a perfect destination for travelers seeking a relaxing beach vacation with plenty of opportunities to explore nature and experience the local culture.

Getting to Phu Quoc

Phu Quoc is accessible by both air and sea. The island has its own international airport with direct flights from major cities in Vietnam and other countries in the region. Alternatively, visitors can take a ferry from the southern mainland city of Rach Gia or from the nearby island of Ha Tien.

Things to do in Phu Quoc

Beach Activities: Phu Quoc is famous for its stunning beaches and clear blue waters, making it a popular destination for swimming, sunbathing, and water sports such as snorkeling and scuba diving. The most popular beaches are Long Beach, Ong Lang Beach, and Sao Beach.

Nature Exploration: The island is also home to a number of beautiful natural sites such as Phu Quoc National Park and Suoi Tranh Waterfall. Visitors can hike through the lush tropical forests, spot a variety of wildlife, and enjoy the breathtaking views.

Island Hopping: Phu Quoc is surrounded by many smaller islands such as An Thoi Archipelago and Hon Thom Island. Visitors can take a boat tour to explore these islands, enjoy their secluded beaches, and witness the island's marine life.

Night Market: For those looking to experience the local culture, Phu Quoc has a vibrant night market where visitors can try a variety of local dishes and buy souvenirs to take home.

Accommodations in Phu Quoc

There are a wide variety of accommodation options in Phu Quoc to suit every traveler's needs and budget. Luxury hotels and resorts are available on

Long Beach and other popular beaches, offering amenities such as swimming pools, spas, and on-site restaurants. Alternatively, there are many budget-friendly guesthouses and hostels scattered throughout the island for backpackers and budget travelers.

Weather in Phu Quoc

The weather in Phu Quoc is warm and sunny throughout the year. The best time to visit is between November and March when the weather is dry and temperatures are more comfortable. The rainy season starts in April and lasts until October, with occasional typhoons and heavy rainstorms.

Conclusion

Phu Quoc is a perfect destination for travelers seeking a relaxing beach vacation with opportunities to explore nature and experience the local culture. With its stunning beaches, crystal-clear waters, lush tropical forests, and vibrant night market, the island is a must-visit for anyone traveling to Vietnam. Whether you're looking for a luxury retreat or a budget-friendly getaway, Phu Quoc has something for everyone.

Chapter 3: Transportation

Planes

Vietnam is a relatively large country, with over 1,000 miles separating its northern and southern regions. As such, flying is a popular mode of transportation for tourists looking to cover long distances in a short amount of time. Vietnam has a well-developed domestic airline network, making it easy to reach even the most remote destinations.

Vietnam Airlines is the country's flagship carrier, operating flights to all major domestic destinations, including Hanoi, Ho Chi Minh City, Da Nang, Nha Trang, and Hue. Other airlines such as Vietjet Air and Bamboo Airways also operate domestic flights, providing passengers with additional options and competitive prices.

The country's two largest airports are Noi Bai International Airport in Hanoi and Tan Son Nhat International Airport in Ho Chi Minh City. Both airports offer a wide range of services and amenities, including currency exchange, ATMs, restaurants, shops, and VIP lounges.

It's important to note that during peak travel seasons, flights can fill up quickly, and prices can rise significantly. Therefore, it's advisable to book your flights well in advance, especially if you're traveling during peak season.

In terms of safety, flying in Vietnam is generally considered safe. All airlines operating in Vietnam meet the safety standards set by the International Air Transport Association (IATA), and the Vietnamese government maintains a robust system of aviation regulations and oversight.

Overall, flying is a fast, convenient, and safe way to travel around Vietnam. However, it's important to do your research and book your flights early to avoid any last-minute price hikes or availability issues.

Trains

Trains are an affordable and comfortable way to travel around Vietnam, offering passengers a chance to see the country's stunning landscapes and picturesque rural villages. Vietnam has an extensive railway network, with trains running from north to south and vice versa.

The most popular train routes for tourists are the Reunification Express, which connects Hanoi in the north to Ho Chi Minh City in the south, and the North-South Express, which runs from Hanoi to Hue and Da Nang.

Trains in Vietnam are divided into several classes, including soft sleeper, hard sleeper, soft seat, and hard seat. Soft sleeper and hard sleeper are the most popular options for long-distance travel, as they offer a comfortable sleeping compartment with air conditioning, clean bedding, and privacy. Soft seat and hard seat are the most economical options and are typically used for shorter journeys.

The ticket prices for trains in Vietnam are relatively affordable, with prices varying depending on the class of travel and the distance covered. It's advisable to book your tickets well in advance, especially during peak travel season, to avoid any last-minute price hikes or availability issues.

Vietnam Railways, the national train operator, operates all train services in Vietnam. You can book train tickets directly through their website or through travel agencies and booking offices located throughout the country.

Trains in Vietnam are generally considered safe, with trains and train stations being well-maintained and monitored by the government. It's important to keep an eye on your belongings, especially during stops at train stations.

In summary, trains are a comfortable and affordable way to travel around Vietnam, offering a chance to see the country's stunning landscapes and rural villages. The train network is extensive, and the different classes of travel provide a range of options for different budgets. It's important to book tickets in advance, keep an eye on your belongings, and enjoy the scenery.

Buses

Buses are a popular mode of transportation in Vietnam, offering an affordable and convenient way to travel around the country. There are many different bus companies that operate throughout Vietnam, with both government-run and private bus services available.

Buses in Vietnam vary in terms of comfort and quality, with some offering air conditioning, reclining seats, and onboard toilets, while others may not have these amenities. Most buses in Vietnam are designed to be used for short to medium distances, with longer journeys typically taken by train or plane.

The prices for buses in Vietnam are generally affordable, with prices varying depending on the distance covered, the type of bus, and the time of year. It's possible to buy tickets directly from bus stations, through travel agencies, or online through booking websites. In some cases, it's also possible to buy tickets onboard the bus.

It's important to note that road safety in Vietnam can be a concern, and accidents involving buses are not uncommon. Some of the smaller bus companies may not adhere to the same safety standards as the larger, more reputable companies, so it's important to do your research and choose a reputable bus company for your journey.

Another consideration is the language barrier, as many of the bus drivers and ticket sellers may not speak English. It's a good idea to have your destination written down in Vietnamese or to use a translation app to help communicate your needs.

In summary, buses are a popular and affordable way to travel around Vietnam, with many different companies and routes available. The quality of buses can vary, so it's important to choose a reputable company and to research the safety standards. Ticket prices are generally affordable, and it's possible to buy tickets directly from bus stations, travel agencies, or online.

Taxis

Taxis are a popular mode of transportation in Vietnam, particularly in major cities like Hanoi and Ho Chi Minh City. They are generally reliable and convenient and can be a good option for getting around quickly, particularly if you are unfamiliar with the local transportation system.

In Vietnam, taxis are typically metered, with the fare calculated based on distance traveled. There are many different taxi companies operating in Vietnam, both government-run and private, with many recognizable international brands like Mai Linh, Vinasun, and Grab also operating in the country.

To use a taxi in Vietnam, you can either flag one down on the street or book one through a ride-hailing app like Grab or Gojek. It's important to make sure that the taxi you are using is licensed and metered, and to confirm the fare before beginning your journey to avoid any potential misunderstandings.

The cost of a taxi ride in Vietnam can vary depending on the distance traveled, the time of day, and the company used. Prices can range from a few dollars for a short journey in a local taxi to several hundred dollars for a longer journey in a luxury vehicle.

One potential issue with taxis in Vietnam is the potential for scams or overcharging. Some taxi drivers may try to negotiate a flat rate or overcharge you for your journey, particularly if you are a foreigner or unfamiliar with the local rates. To avoid this, it's a good idea to do your research and have an idea of what the standard rates are before beginning your journey. You can also use a ride-hailing app, which will give you an upfront price estimate and ensure that the fare is metered and transparent.

In summary, taxis are a popular and convenient way to travel in Vietnam, particularly in major cities. They are typically metered, with prices calculated based on distance traveled. There are many different taxi companies operating in Vietnam, and it's important to choose a licensed and reputable company to avoid potential scams or overcharging. Ride-hailing apps like Grab and Gojek can also be a good option for ensuring transparent pricing and reliable service.

Motorbikes

Motorbikes are a popular mode of transportation in Vietnam, especially for locals and backpackers. They offer a sense of freedom and flexibility to explore the country at your own pace. However, it's important to note that motorbikes can also be dangerous, especially for inexperienced riders.

To rent a motorbike in Vietnam, you'll need a valid driver's license, either from your home country or an international driver's license. You'll also need to provide a deposit and fill out some paperwork with the rental company. The cost of renting a motorbike varies depending on the type of bike and the length of the rental period.

It's important to wear a helmet while riding a motorbike in Vietnam, as it's required by law and can save your life in case of an accident. You should also wear protective clothing, such as long pants and closed-toe shoes, to reduce the risk of injury.

When driving a motorbike in Vietnam, it's important to be aware of the traffic rules and customs. Traffic in Vietnam can be chaotic, with many motorbikes and cars on the road at once. You should always drive defensively and be prepared for sudden stops and turns. It's also important to be aware of the road conditions, which can vary greatly depending on the location and weather.

One thing to note is that some areas of Vietnam require a special permit to drive a motorbike, especially if you plan to drive outside of the main cities. These permits can be obtained through local travel agencies or the police.

In terms of fuel, gas stations are common in urban areas, but they can be harder to find in rural areas. You can purchase gasoline in plastic bottles from local vendors, but it's important to check the quality of the fuel before purchasing.

Overall, motorbikes can be a fun and exciting way to travel in Vietnam, but they should be approached with caution and respect for the rules of the road. It's important to have a good understanding of how to ride a motorbike safely before embarking on a long trip.

Tips for using public transportation

Here are some tips for using public transportation in Vietnam:

- Plan ahead: Before you travel, research the routes, schedules, and fares of public transportation. This can save you time and money and make your travel smoother.

- Get a map: Get a map of the public transportation system in the city you're traveling in. This can help you navigate your way around and find your destination easily.

- Be aware of rush hour: Public transportation can get very crowded during rush hour, so plan accordingly. You may want to avoid traveling during peak hours or be prepared for a crowded and potentially uncomfortable journey.

- Be aware of scams: Unfortunately, scams targeting tourists are not uncommon on public transportation in Vietnam. Be aware of pickpocketing and other scams and keep an eye on your belongings.

- Be respectful: Vietnamese people are generally friendly and polite, and it is important to return the courtesy. Offer your seat to the elderly or disabled, don't make a lot of noise, and don't eat or drink on public transportation.

- Buy tickets from official vendors: Be sure to buy your tickets from official vendors or ticket counters, as buying tickets from unofficial sources can be risky and may result in higher fares or even fraud.

- Use common sense: Finally, use common sense when using public transportation in Vietnam. Be aware of your surroundings, be mindful of traffic, and stay safe.

Driving in Vietnam

Driving in Vietnam can be an adventure in itself. The roads are busy and often chaotic, and traffic laws are not always followed. For this reason, many visitors to Vietnam choose to use public transportation rather than drive themselves.

However, if you do choose to rent a car or motorbike and drive in Vietnam, there are some important things to keep in mind. Here are some tips to help you navigate the roads safely:

- Get an International Driving Permit: To legally drive in Vietnam, you will need an International Driving Permit (IDP). This is a document that translates your driver's license into different languages and is recognized in many countries around the world.

- Follow local driving customs: Traffic in Vietnam can be chaotic, and drivers often ignore traffic laws. Follow the flow of traffic and be cautious when turning or changing lanes.

- Wear a helmet: If you plan to ride a motorbike or scooter, it's important to wear a helmet. Not only is it the law, but it can also save your life in the event of an accident.

- Avoid driving at night: It's best to avoid driving at night in Vietnam, as many roads are poorly lit and it can be difficult to see other drivers or obstacles.

- Stay alert: Keep an eye out for pedestrians, bicycles, and other motorbikes, which are often weaving in and out of traffic.

- Be patient: Traffic can be slow in Vietnam, especially in major cities like Hanoi and Ho Chi Minh City. Be patient and give yourself plenty of time to get to your destination.

- Use GPS or maps: If you're driving in a new city or area, use a GPS or maps to help you navigate the roads.

- Watch out for scams: Some rental companies or individuals may try to scam you by charging you for damages that you didn't cause. Take photos of the vehicle before you rent it and inspect it thoroughly to avoid any misunderstandings.

- Don't drink and drive: This should go without saying, but it's important to never drink and drive. Vietnam has strict penalties for drunk driving, and it's simply not worth the risk.

By following these tips, you can stay safe and enjoy the freedom of driving in Vietnam. However, if you're not comfortable with the idea of driving in such chaotic traffic, there are plenty of other transportation options available.

Hiring a private driver

Hiring a private driver is a popular and convenient option for tourists who want to explore Vietnam. Private drivers can offer a more personalized experience and can take you to places that may not be easily accessible through public transportation. Here are some tips on hiring a private driver in Vietnam:

- Research and compare prices: It's important to do some research and compare prices before hiring a private driver. Prices can vary depending on the location, distance, and duration of the trip. You can check online reviews or ask for recommendations from friends or hotels.

- Negotiate the price: In Vietnam, it's common to negotiate the price before hiring a private driver. Make sure to agree on a price before the trip to avoid any misunderstandings.

- Check the vehicle: Make sure to check the condition of the vehicle before hiring a private driver. It's important that the vehicle is safe and comfortable for the trip.

- Agree on the itinerary: Make sure to agree on the itinerary with the driver before the trip. This will help avoid any misunderstandings or unexpected stops during the trip.

- Communicate clearly: It's important to communicate clearly with the driver during the trip. Make sure to let the driver know if you need to make any stops or if you have any special requests.

Hiring a private driver can be a great way to explore Vietnam, but it's important to take the necessary precautions and do your research before the trip.

Chapter 4: Accommodation

Hotels

Vietnam has a wide variety of accommodations to fit different budgets and preferences. From luxury hotels to budget-friendly hostels, there is something for everyone.

Some of the best hotels in Vietnam include:

- The Reverie Saigon: Located in Ho Chi Minh City, this hotel is known for its opulent design and exceptional service. It features 12 different types of rooms and suites, six dining options, a spa, and a rooftop pool.
- The Four Seasons Resort the Nam Hai: Situated in Hoi An, this beachfront resort offers luxurious villas and suites with private pools, a spa, and three beachfront pools.
- Sofitel Legend Metropole Hanoi: This historic hotel is located in the heart of Hanoi and offers French colonial-style rooms and suites, as well as five dining options, a bar, a spa, and a heated outdoor pool.

- InterContinental Danang Sun Peninsula Resort: Set in the hills above the picturesque Son Tra Peninsula, this resort offers stunning views of the ocean and lush greenery. It has luxurious rooms and suites, private pools, and a variety of dining options.
- Amanoi: Situated on a secluded hillside overlooking Vinh Hy Bay, this peaceful and luxurious resort offers spacious villas with private pools, a spa, a fitness center, and two dining options.

When choosing a hotel in Vietnam, it's important to consider the location, amenities, and price. Many hotels offer breakfast and free Wi-Fi, so be sure to check the amenities included in your booking.

My personal preference for a hotel in Vietnam would be the InterContinental Danang Sun Peninsula Resort. The resort's stunning location and luxurious accommodations make for a truly memorable experience. Plus, the variety of dining options and exceptional service make it a great choice for a relaxing and indulgent vacation.

Hostels

Hostels are a great option for budget-conscious travelers looking for affordable accommodation in Vietnam. There are many hostels throughout the country, with options ranging from basic dorm rooms to private rooms with en-suite bathrooms. Most hostels in Vietnam offer shared facilities such as kitchens, lounges, and laundry rooms, making them a popular choice for backpackers and solo travelers.

Some of the best hostels in Vietnam include the following:

- Vietnam Backpacker Hostels - Hanoi: This hostel chain is popular with backpackers and offers a range of accommodation options in Hanoi, including dorms and private rooms. The hostel also offers tours and activities for guests.
- The Common Room Project - Ho Chi Minh City: This trendy hostel offers a unique blend of Vietnamese and European design and is located in the heart of Ho Chi Minh City. The hostel offers private rooms and shared dorms, as well as a rooftop bar and lounge.

- The Hanoi Social Hostel - Hanoi: This popular hostel offers private rooms and dorms and is located in the heart of Hanoi's Old Quarter. The hostel also offers a range of tours and activities for guests, including street food tours and cooking classes.
- Capsule Hanoi Hostel - Hanoi: This stylish hostel offers unique capsule-style dorms with individual TVs and power outlets, as well as private rooms. The hostel is located in Hanoi's Old Quarter and offers a range of facilities, including a rooftop terrace and bar.

When booking a hostel in Vietnam, it's important to keep in mind that standards can vary widely, and it's always a good idea to read reviews and research the hostel before booking. It's also a good idea to book in advance during peak travel periods, as hostels can fill up quickly.

In terms of pricing, hostels in Vietnam can range from as little as $5 USD per night for a basic dorm room to $30 USD per night for a private room with an en-suite bathroom. Prices are generally higher in larger cities and popular tourist destinations.

Vietnam Backpacker Hostels in Hanoi is the hostel that I would recommend to other travelers visiting Vietnam. This hostel was great for me because of the kind and helpful staff, the social environment, and the accessible location in the center of the Old Quarter. The fact that the hostel provides guests with a variety of excursions and activities made it simple to interact with other tourists and discover the local area. The dormitory rooms were simple but comfortable, and the communal bathrooms and kitchen were spotless and well-maintained across the whole building. After a long day of sight-seeing, guests may unwind at the hostel's rooftop bar, where they can have a drink while taking in the view of the city below. In general, I would strongly suggest Vietnam Backpacker Hostels to any tourists who are on a tight budget and are searching for a hostel experience in Hanoi that is both fun and sociable.

Homestays

Homestays are becoming more popular among tourists who are interested in gaining a deeper and more genuine understanding of the culture and way of life in Vietnam. Homestays provide the chance to stay with a local family and get firsthand knowledge of the routines, rituals, and practices that are unique to the community. This may be a wonderful opportunity to go off the main path, get some insight into the culture of the area, and have some home-cooked meals.

Homestays are accessible in all parts of Vietnam, although they are especially common in the country's more rural regions and its smaller cities. The majority of homestays provide basic lodging, most of the time in a house designed in the traditional manner, and guests share utilities like baths and kitchens. It is essential to verify this information with the host prior to making a reservation. Some may offer more contemporary conveniences such as air conditioning, Wi-Fi, and hot water.

The cost of homestays may vary greatly based on factors such as the degree of comfort offered and the conveniences that are provided. Homestays, on the other hand, often provide more reasonable rates than hotels, with costs typically ranging from around $10 to $50 per night, per individual. It is crucial to bear in mind that certain homestays may not offer the same degree of cleanliness, privacy, or security as a hotel. As a result, before making a reservation, it is vital to read reviews and conduct some research.

When you book a homestay, it is vital to bear in mind that you will be living in someone else's home.

Because of this, it is essential to be respectful of the house rules as well as the host's way of life. This may include taking off your shoes before entering the building, adhering to a certain dress code, or respecting a variety of other rituals and practices. It is essential that you get in touch with your host before you arrive at the homestay in order to confirm your reservation, inquire about any particular requirements or wishes you may have, and obtain instructions to the location of the homestay.

The Mai Chau Ecolodge, which is situated in the Mai Chau valley and is around three hours' travel time from Hanoi, is the homestay option that I recommend the most. The Ecolodge has stunning lodgings in a classic design, along with 21st-century conveniences such as private bathrooms, air conditioning, and wireless internet access. The setting is really breathtaking, as it is surrounded by rice fields, woods, and mountains, and there are many chances for engaging in outdoor activities like as hiking, bicycling, and participating in cultural excursions. The wait staff is very warm and welcoming, and the cuisine is great, since it is prepared with fresh products from the surrounding area. The Mai Chau Ecolodge offers accommodations for a nightly rate of around $50 per person, which includes both breakfast and supper.

Tips for booking accommodation

Here are some tips for booking accommodation in Vietnam:

- Research your options: Do some research and compare different accommodation options, such as hotels, hostels, and homestays. Read reviews from other travelers to get a sense of the pros and cons of each option.
- Consider the location: Make sure to choose accommodation in a location that suits your needs. If you're looking for a peaceful retreat, for example, you might prefer to stay outside of the city center. On the other hand, if you want to be in the heart of the action, you'll want to choose a hotel or hostel in a central location.
- Check the amenities: Look for accommodation with the amenities you need, such as free Wi-Fi, air conditioning, or a swimming pool. Make sure to check the room sizes, as well as the number of beds and

bathrooms, to ensure that the accommodation is suitable for your group.

- Book in advance: In peak season, accommodation can get booked up quickly, so it's best to book well in advance. If you're planning to visit during a major holiday or festival, make sure to book even further ahead.
- Check cancellation policies: Before making a booking, check the cancellation policy. Some accommodation options may offer free cancellation up to a certain point, while others may have stricter policies. Make sure to understand the cancellation policy so that you can make changes if needed.
- Keep an eye on price: Finally, keep an eye on the price when booking accommodation. Prices can fluctuate, so consider setting up price alerts or checking back frequently to ensure you get the best deal.

When it comes to my personal preference for accommodation in Vietnam, I particularly enjoyed staying at homestays. They offer an authentic cultural experience, and often provide opportunities to interact with local people and learn about their way of life. I found them to be cozy, comfortable, and very affordable. One homestay I particularly enjoyed was in Sapa, where the host family cooked us delicious local meals and took us on a trek through the rice terraces.

Chapter 5: Food and Drink

Vietnamese cuisine

Vietnamese cuisine is a vibrant and diverse culinary tradition, with a long and rich history. The cuisine is known for its use of fresh herbs and vegetables, along with a wide variety of spices and sauces, which contribute to the unique and delicious flavors of Vietnamese dishes.

The History of Vietnamese Cuisine Vietnamese cuisine has been heavily influenced by the country's long history of colonization, occupation, and trade with neighboring countries. The Chinese, French, and Japanese have all had a significant impact on the development of Vietnamese cuisine. The Chinese introduced rice cultivation and the use of chopsticks, while the French introduced pastries, coffee, and other western culinary traditions.

Vietnamese cuisine is also heavily influenced by the country's geography, which spans a wide range of landscapes, from the lush Mekong Delta to the rugged mountains of the north. As a result, different regions of the country have developed their own unique culinary traditions, using local ingredients and flavors.

Common Ingredients and Dishes One of the most important ingredients in Vietnamese cuisine is rice, which is a staple in the country's diet. It is used in many dishes, including pho (a traditional noodle soup), com tam (broken rice), and banh mi (a sandwich made with a baguette).

Fish sauce is another essential ingredient in Vietnamese cuisine. It is used to season many dishes, including stir-fries, noodle soups, and dipping sauces. Other popular ingredients include lemongrass, lime, garlic, ginger, and chili peppers.

Pho is perhaps the most famous Vietnamese dish, consisting of a rich, aromatic broth made with beef or chicken, along with rice noodles, bean sprouts, and herbs. Other popular dishes include banh mi, a sandwich made with pork, pickled vegetables, and fresh herbs; bun cha, grilled pork served with noodles and fresh herbs; and ca kho to, caramelized fish simmered in a clay pot with spices and vegetables.

Regional Cuisines Vietnam's regional cuisines are diverse and complex, with each region having its own unique culinary traditions. In the north, the cuisine is heavily influenced by China, and features dishes like bun cha and pho. The central region is known for its spicy and sour flavors, and dishes like bun bo Hue, a spicy beef noodle soup, and com hen, a dish made with baby clams and rice.

In the south, the cuisine is influenced by Cambodia and Thailand, and features sweet and spicy flavors, as well as a wide variety of herbs and spices. Dishes like banh xeo, a savory pancake filled with shrimp, pork, and bean sprouts, and hu tieu, a noodle soup made with seafood and pork, are popular in the south.

In addition to these regional cuisines, there are also many dishes that are specific to certain areas or villages. For example, cao lau is a noodle dish that is only found in the central city of Hoi An, and banh cuon is a steamed rice noodle dish that is popular in the north.

Conclusion Vietnamese cuisine is a complex and diverse culinary tradition, with a rich history and unique flavors. Whether you are a food lover or just looking to try something new, there is no shortage of delicious and authentic Vietnamese dishes to explore. From pho to banh mi to bun cha, there is something for everyone to enjoy.

Street food

Street food is a quintessential part of the Vietnamese culinary experience, and for many visitors to Vietnam, it is one of the highlights of their trip. Vietnamese street food is diverse, delicious, and affordable, and it offers a glimpse into the everyday lives of locals. However, it's important to keep in mind a few tips to ensure you have a safe and enjoyable experience with street food.

The best street food in Vietnam can be found in the major cities, such as Hanoi, Ho Chi Minh City, and Hue, as well as in smaller towns and villages throughout the country. Some of the most popular street food dishes include pho (a type of noodle soup), banh mi (a Vietnamese sandwich), bun cha (grilled pork with noodles), and banh xeo (a savory pancake).

When looking for street food, it's important to seek out places where the locals eat. These places are likely to have the freshest and most authentic food, and they also tend to be the most affordable. Look for street vendors with a steady stream of customers, as this is a sign that their food is popular and of good quality.

Another tip when eating street food in Vietnam is to be cautious of scams. While most street food vendors are honest and trustworthy, some may try to overcharge tourists or give them less food than they paid for. Be sure to confirm the price before ordering and watch as the vendor prepares your food to ensure that you receive what you paid for.

It's also important to keep in mind basic food safety when eating street food in Vietnam. Look for food that is cooked to order and served hot, as this is less likely to harbor harmful bacteria. Avoid food that has been sitting out for long periods of time or food that looks old or stale.

In summary, Vietnamese street food is a must-try for any foodie visiting the country. Just remember to look for popular vendors, confirm the price before ordering, and keep basic food safety in mind. By following these tips, you can enjoy the delicious and affordable street food of Vietnam without any worries.

Vegetarian and vegan options

Vietnamese cuisine is known for its use of fresh herbs and vegetables, making it an excellent destination for vegetarians and vegans. In fact, many of the traditional Vietnamese dishes are already plant-based, such as pho noodle soup made with vegetables or tofu instead of meat.

Some of the most popular vegetarian and vegan dishes include:

- Pho Chay - a vegetarian version of the famous pho noodle soup made with vegetable broth, tofu, and various vegetables.
- Banh Mi Chay - a vegan version of the popular Vietnamese sandwich filled with tofu, mushrooms, and a variety of fresh vegetables.
- Com Chay - a vegetarian version of the Vietnamese rice dish, usually made with fried tofu, vegetables, and served with a side of pickled vegetables.
- Goi Cuon Chay - vegetarian summer rolls filled with tofu, vermicelli noodles, and fresh vegetables.

There are also many vegetarian and vegan restaurants throughout Vietnam, especially in the major cities such as Hanoi and Ho Chi Minh City.

These restaurants serve a variety of dishes that are specifically made for vegetarians and vegans.

When it comes to street food, it's important to be cautious as a vegetarian or vegan since many dishes may contain meat broth or fish sauce. It's best to ask the vendor if they have any vegetarian or vegan options available, and to watch for the ingredients used in each dish.

Overall, Vietnam is a great destination for vegetarians and vegans, with many options available both in restaurants and on the street.

Drinking culture

There is a wide variety of traditional and contemporary alcoholic beverages available in Vietnam, contributing to the country's robust and varied drinking culture. Drinking plays a significant role in Vietnamese culture due to the fact that Vietnamese people like socializing and celebrating with alcoholic beverages. In Vietnam, you may sample a wide variety of tasty and one-of-a-kind beverages, from rice wine to coffee.

Rice wine, also known as "ruou," is one of the most well-known alcoholic beverages in Vietnam and is considered to be a traditional beverage. Rice wine is a very robust and alcoholic beverage that is produced by the fermentation of rice using yeast. It is typical for it to be eaten during big festivities and ceremonies like weddings, funerals, and other important events. Rice wine is a popular alcoholic beverage in Vietnam, and the country produces a large number of distinct variations of the beverage.

Beer is another common alcoholic beverage in Vietnam. Beer consumption is quickly becoming more popular in Vietnam, and consumers may choose from a wide variety of domestic and foreign brands. One of the most well-liked and inexpensive choices available is Bia Hoi beer, which is made right in the neighborhood. It is often poured from a tap in little plastic cups and is at its most enjoyable when paired with other snacks or cuisine sold on the street.

Moreover, Vietnam is well-known for the culture around its coffee. Coffee from Vietnam has a reputation for having a robust flavor, and it is often consumed with condensed milk or over ice. Egg coffee is a creamy and rich beverage that is produced by combining egg yolks, sugar, and condensed milk. It is one of the most well-known and distinctive varieties of coffee. This beverage can be traced back to Hanoi and is an absolute must-try for everyone who like coffee.

In addition to coffee drinks and alcoholic beverages, visitors visiting Vietnam may sample a wide variety of non-alcoholic drinks as well. A common option is sugarcane juice, which is a drink that is both sweet and refreshing and is created by pressing sugarcane. On a day when it's particularly warm, drinking coconut water, fresh fruit juice, or a smoothie is not only easy to get but also an excellent method to cool down.

Although though drinking is an integral part of Vietnamese culture, it is essential to be vigilant while buying alcoholic beverages because of the prevalence of frauds. It's possible that certain restaurants and pubs overpay for drinks or provide phony alcoholic beverages. If you want to avoid falling into these traps, the easiest approach to protect yourself is to conduct some research or ask for tips.

In conclusion, the drinking culture of Vietnam is very varied and has a wide variety of beverages that are both distinctive and delectable. Everyone may find something to their liking, whether it be an old-fashioned rice wine or a contemporary coffee drink. While buying alcoholic beverages, it is imperative that you exercise extreme caution and stay away from cons.

Chapter 6: Activities and Attractions

Cultural attractions

Vietnam is a country rich in culture, with numerous historical and cultural attractions. Here are some of the top cultural attractions in Vietnam:

- Hoi An Ancient Town - Located in central Vietnam, Hoi An is a well-preserved example of an ancient trading port. The town is known for its well-preserved architecture, including historic homes, pagodas, and temples. The best time to visit is in the early morning or late afternoon, as the town can get quite crowded during the day.
- Ho Chi Minh Mausoleum - Located in Hanoi, the Ho Chi Minh Mausoleum is the final resting place of the Vietnamese revolutionary leader, Ho Chi Minh. Visitors can pay their respects to the former leader but should dress conservatively and be prepared for long lines.
- Hue Imperial City - Located in central Vietnam, Hue was the seat of the Nguyen Dynasty and is home to a walled fortress and a complex of royal palaces and temples. The

best time to visit is in the early morning, as the site can get quite hot and crowded during the day.

- Cu Chi Tunnels - Located just outside of Ho Chi Minh City, the Cu Chi Tunnels were used by the Viet Cong during the Vietnam War. Visitors can explore the tunnels and learn about the history of the war.
- My Son Sanctuary - Located near Hoi An, My Son Sanctuary is a complex of Hindu temples that date back to the 4th century. The temples were heavily damaged during the Vietnam War but have since been restored and are now a UNESCO World Heritage Site.
- Imperial Tombs of Hue - The tombs of the Nguyen Dynasty emperors are located on the outskirts of Hue and are known for their impressive architecture and beautiful gardens.
- Temple of Literature - Located in Hanoi, the Temple of Literature was built in the 11th century and is dedicated to Confucius. It is Vietnam's oldest university and is considered one of the country's most important cultural sites.
- War Remnants Museum - Located in Ho Chi Minh City, the War Remnants Museum is a sobering look at the Vietnam War from the

perspective of the Vietnamese. Visitors can see exhibits and artifacts related to the war, including photographs, weapons, and other items.

- Phong Nha-Ke Bang National Park - Located in central Vietnam, Phong Nha-Ke Bang National Park is home to a network of caves that are among the largest in the world. Visitors can take guided tours of the caves and learn about their formation and history.
- Cao Dai Temple - Located in Tay Ninh, the Cao Dai Temple is the center of the Cao Dai religion, which combines elements of Buddhism, Taoism, Confucianism, and Christianity. Visitors can witness the colorful and elaborate rituals and ceremonies of this unique religion.

The best time to visit these cultural attractions varies, but generally the dry season from November to March is the most comfortable for travelers. However, it's important to note that some attractions may be closed or have limited hours during national holidays or special events. It's also important to dress conservatively and respectfully when visiting religious sites or mausoleums.

Natural attractions

Vietnam is a country blessed with natural beauty, from the stunning coastline to majestic mountains, vast green rice fields, and dense jungles. There are several natural attractions worth visiting, and below are some of the most popular ones:

- Halong Bay: One of Vietnam's most iconic sights is Halong Bay, a UNESCO World Heritage Site located in the Gulf of Tonkin. Halong Bay features over 1,600 limestone islets and karst formations, which create a breathtaking seascape. The best time to visit is from September to November or from March to May, and prices for tours and cruises vary depending on the duration and type of vessel.
- Phong Nha-Ke Bang National Park: Located in central Vietnam, Phong Nha-Ke Bang National Park is a UNESCO World Heritage Site renowned for its karst mountains and underground rivers and caves. The park is home to over 300 caves, including the world's largest cave, Son Doong. The best time to visit is from February to August, and prices vary depending on the tour or activity.
- Sapa: Sapa is a highland town located in the northwest of Vietnam and is known for its

terraced rice fields, unique ethnic cultures, and cool climate. The best time to visit is from September to November or from March to May, and prices for tours or activities vary.

- Phu Quoc Island: Phu Quoc Island is the largest island in Vietnam, located in the Gulf of Thailand. The island is famous for its white sandy beaches, coral reefs, and tropical forests. The best time to visit is from November to March, and prices vary depending on the accommodation and activities.

- Mekong Delta: The Mekong Delta is a vast network of rivers and waterways that flows into the South China Sea. The delta is known for its fertile land, traditional floating markets, and unique river culture. The best time to visit is from November to April, and prices vary depending on the tour or activity.

When visiting these natural attractions, it's essential to respect the environment and be mindful of any entrance fees or conservation fees required to enter certain areas. It's also important to use reputable tour operators and guides to ensure your safety and a memorable experience.

Adventure activities

Vietnam is a country with a wide range of adventure activities available for tourists to enjoy. From hiking to kayaking, from rock climbing to cycling, there is something for everyone. Here are some of the top adventure activities in Vietnam:

- Trekking and hiking - Vietnam has some of the most stunning landscapes in Southeast Asia, and trekking and hiking are great ways to explore these natural wonders. Popular destinations for trekking and hiking include Sapa, Ba Be National Park, and Cat Ba Island.
- Rock climbing - With towering limestone cliffs, Vietnam is a great destination for rock climbing. Halong Bay and Cat Ba Island are popular destinations for rock climbing, with routes for all skill levels.
- Cycling - Vietnam is a great country to explore on two wheels. From the bustling streets of Hanoi to the peaceful countryside of the Mekong Delta, there are cycling routes for all levels of riders.
- Kayaking and canoeing - Vietnam has an extensive coastline and a network of rivers and lakes that are perfect for kayaking and

canoeing. Some popular destinations for kayaking and canoeing include Halong Bay, Ninh Binh, and the Mekong Delta.

- Scuba diving and snorkeling - Vietnam is home to some of the most diverse marine life in Southeast Asia, making it a great destination for scuba diving and snorkeling. Popular diving spots include Nha Trang and Phu Quoc.
- Zip lining - For a thrilling adventure, try zip lining in the hills and forests of Vietnam. The best zip lining experiences can be found in Da Lat and Phong Nha.
- Bungee jumping - For the ultimate adrenaline rush, bungee jumping is available in certain locations in Vietnam, including Ho Chi Minh City and Hanoi.

The best time to participate in these activities varies depending on the location and activity. For example, trekking and hiking in Sapa is best during the dry season from September to November or from March to May, while kayaking in Halong Bay is best during the summer months from June to August.

Prices for these activities vary depending on the location and the type of activity. Some activities, such as hiking and cycling, can be done independently, while others require a tour operator or guide. It is always important to research and book with a reputable tour operator to ensure safety and a quality experience.

Overall, Vietnam offers a wide range of adventure activities that are sure to satisfy any traveler seeking a bit of excitement and outdoor adventure.

Shopping

Shopping in Vietnam can be a fun and exciting experience. The country offers a wide variety of shopping options, from bustling markets to high-end malls. Here are some of the best places to shop in Vietnam:

- Ben Thanh Market (Ho Chi Minh City): This is one of the oldest and most popular markets in Ho Chi Minh City, offering a wide range of goods from clothing and souvenirs to fresh produce and street food. It's a great place to haggle for a bargain.
- Dong Xuan Market (Hanoi): Located in the heart of Hanoi's Old Quarter, Dong Xuan Market is a large, multi-level market selling everything from clothing and electronics to housewares and traditional handicrafts.

- Hoi An Night Market (Hoi An): This colorful and bustling market opens every night in the ancient town of Hoi An, selling souvenirs, clothing, and local street food. The market is especially beautiful at night, with lanterns and lights adding to the atmosphere.
- Saigon Centre (Ho Chi Minh City): For high-end shopping, Saigon Centre is a great option. This modern shopping center features international brands and luxury items, as well as a cinema and restaurants.
- Vincom Center (Hanoi and Ho Chi Minh City): Another option for upscale shopping, Vincom Center has multiple locations in Hanoi and Ho Chi Minh City. It offers luxury brands, electronics, and entertainment options.
- Lotte Mart (Hanoi and Ho Chi Minh City): Lotte Mart is a popular supermarket chain in Vietnam, selling groceries, clothing, electronics, and household items. The stores also have food courts and play areas for kids.
- The Night Market (Phu Quoc): This market is located on the island of Phu Quoc and is a great place to shop for souvenirs and beachwear. The market is open every night, and visitors can also enjoy street food and live music.

When it comes to what to buy, Vietnam is famous for its silk, lacquerware, and traditional handicrafts like pottery and wood carvings. Other popular souvenirs include conical hats, coffee, and tea. Be sure to haggle for a good price when shopping in markets, and keep in mind that bargaining is expected in many places.

Nightlife

The nightlife scene in Vietnam is bustling and diversified, with alternatives that may cater to a variety of preferences and price points. Those who are searching for a night out have a wide variety of options to choose from around the nation, which range from underground music venues to rooftop pubs with breath-taking views.

There is a diverse selection of bars and nightclubs to be found in the main cities of Vietnam, such as Ho Chi Minh City, Hanoi, and Da Nang. These establishments vary from sophisticated lounges to laid-back dive bars. When residents and visitors mix and mingle while taking in the sights and sounds of the nightlife, the environment may have a vibrant and exciting vibe.

Karaoke is often ranked as one of the most popular ways to spend a night out in Vietnam. Karaoke bars may be located all across the United States, and they provide patrons an entertaining and distinctive way to spend the evening. In many of these venues, you may get a private area where you and your pals can belt out your favorite songs without the whole bar hearing you.

Rooftop bars and upmarket clubs abound in Vietnam, making the country an ideal destination for those seeking an affluent travel experience. These pubs often host live music and are known for their inventive drink menus, in addition to providing breath-taking views of the city.

Vietnam is home to a booming nightlife scene that includes bars and nightclubs, as well as a vibrant street food culture that comes to life after dark. Night markets are a favorite destination for foodies because they provide a diverse selection of street food, ranging from seafood and pho to unusual delicacies like fried insects and snake wine. Night markets are also a great place to get unique souvenirs.

Evenings in Vietnam are filled with a variety of live events and cultural performances, which are perfect for anybody who has an interest in the performing arts. These vary from traditional displays including water puppets to modern dance acts, and they provide a wonderful opportunity to get exposure to the culture of the area.

It is essential to be aware that Vietnam has stringent rules against the use of drugs as well as the possession of drugs, and the punishments may be harsh. When out experiencing the nightlife in Vietnam, it is in your best interest to abstain from using any form of illegal or prescription medication.

In general, the nightlife culture in Vietnam is broad, vibrant, and accommodating to people of varying preferences and financial means. Everyone will find something to their liking, whether it is the laid-back atmosphere of the street food markets or the upmarket atmosphere of the rooftop bars.

Chapter 7: Local Customs and Etiquette

Greetings and language

Vietnamese is the official language of Vietnam, and while many people in major cities and tourist destinations may speak some English, it's always helpful to know some basic Vietnamese phrases to make your travels easier and more enjoyable. Here are some common greetings and phrases to get you started:

- Xin chào (sin chow) - Hello
- Tạm biệt (tahm bee-yet) - Goodbye
- Cảm ơn (kahm uhn) - Thank you.
- Không có gì (khom koh zee) - You're welcome.
- Xin lỗi (sin loy) - Sorry/excuse me
- Tôi không hiểu (toy khom hyoo) - I don't understand.
- Tôi muốn (toy moon) - I want.

- Bao nhiêu tiền? (Bow nyew tee-en) - How much does it cost?
- Cho tôi xin (choy toy sin) - Can I have...?

Learning these basic phrases will make a big difference in your interactions with locals and show that you respect and appreciate their culture. Vietnamese is a tonal language, so it's important to pay attention to your intonation when speaking. If you're not sure how to pronounce a word, don't be afraid to ask a local for help - they'll likely appreciate your efforts to learn their language.

In addition to Vietnamese, many people in Vietnam also speak French and Chinese, particularly in older generations. English is becoming increasingly common, especially among younger people and those working in the tourism industry.

Overall, taking the time to learn some basic Vietnamese phrases will enhance your travel experience and help you better connect with the local culture.

Dress code

Vietnam is a country that values modesty and respect, and as such, dressing appropriately is important when traveling here. It's important to keep in mind that Vietnam is a conservative country, especially in rural areas and temples, so revealing clothing or provocative attire is not acceptable.

Here are some guidelines to follow when it comes to dressing in Vietnam:

- Covering Shoulders and Knees: It is recommended to cover your shoulders and knees when visiting temples, mosques, pagodas, and other religious sites in Vietnam. You should wear long pants or skirts that fall below the knee, and shirts with sleeves that cover your shoulders.
- Lightweight and Breathable Clothing: The weather in Vietnam is hot and humid, so it's important to wear lightweight and breathable clothing. Cotton or linen fabric is ideal as they are light and airy and keep you cool.
- Footwear: Flip-flops or sandals are perfect for the hot and humid weather in Vietnam, but when visiting temples, you may need to remove your shoes, so it is a good idea to bring socks. It's also important to wear

comfortable shoes for walking as some areas may be uneven or slippery.

- Conservative Clothing: It's important to avoid wearing anything too tight, too short, or too revealing. Low-cut tops or short skirts should be avoided, especially in rural areas, and when traveling to more conservative parts of the country.
- Formal Attire: It's not always necessary to dress formally in Vietnam, but it's a good idea to bring at least one formal outfit for special occasions, such as weddings or business meetings.

It's also important to note that Vietnam is a country with a deep sense of cultural and historical pride, and as such, it's important to respect the local customs and traditions. Dressing appropriately shows respect to the culture and the people, and it can help you to have a more enjoyable experience during your travels.

Tipping

Tipping is not a widely practiced custom in Vietnam; nonetheless, it is becoming more customary in locations frequented by tourists. Tipping is not something that is required at restaurants or cafés, but it is appreciated if you believe the service that you received to be above and above. It is common practice at high-end hotels and restaurants to leave a tip of between 5 and 10 percent, particularly if a service fee has been included to the bill.

You should not feel forced to leave gratuities for other service providers, such as taxi drivers or tour guides, since this is not the tradition, and you should not expect to get anything in return for your generosity. On the other hand, if you consider that they have provided you with great service, a tip of any size is always appreciated, regardless of the amount that you choose to give.

It is essential that you bear in mind that if you are taking part in a tour, the guide may ask you for a tip at the end of the trip. This is something that you should prepare yourself for. This happens more often on group trips, and the amount that is normally requested from each person is just a few dollars at most. It is completely up to you to decide whether or not you would want to leave a tip for your tour guide in Vietnam; however, keep in mind that many tour guides in Vietnam are not paid very well, and even a little tip may make a significant difference for them.

Tipping is often not expected in Vietnam, and if it is done at all, it is seen more as a gesture of goodwill than as a necessary part of service. If you would want to leave a tip, it is OK to provide a little amount; nevertheless, it is not needed that you leave a sizable sum as a gratuity.

Bargaining

Bargaining is a common practice in Vietnam, especially in markets and small shops. As a tourist, it is important to know how to bargain to avoid being overcharged. Here are some tips for bargaining in Vietnam:

- Start with a smile and a friendly greeting. This helps to establish a good relationship with the seller, which can increase your chances of getting a good deal.

- Know the market value of the item you want to buy. Do some research beforehand to know the rough price range of the item you are interested in. This will help you to negotiate better and avoid being ripped off.
- Don't be afraid to walk away. If the seller is not willing to meet your price, be prepared to walk away. Often, the seller will call you back and offer a better price.
- Be polite and respectful. Avoid being rude or aggressive during the bargaining process. It is important to show respect to the seller and remember that bargaining is part of the Vietnamese culture.
- Offer a fair price. It is important to offer a fair price for the item you are interested in. Don't offer too low of a price, as this can be seen as disrespectful.
- Consider the quality of the item. Take into consideration the quality of the item you are interested in. If it is of high quality, it may be worth paying a little extra.
- Buy in bulk. If you are interested in purchasing several items from the same seller, consider bargaining for a bulk discount.

One personal experience I had while bargaining in Vietnam was when I was looking to buy a traditional Vietnamese hat as a souvenir. I found a small shop in the market that sold them and began to bargain with the seller. We went back and forth for a while, and I was eventually able to get the price down to a level that I was happy with. As I was about to pay, the seller suddenly raised the price and said that the original price we had agreed on was too low. I was taken aback but remembered to stay polite and respectful. I calmly explained that we had already agreed on a price, and after a few more minutes of back and forth, the seller eventually agreed to sell me the hat at the original price we had agreed on. It was a good reminder to stay calm and respectful during the bargaining process, even if the seller tries to change the price at the last minute.

Dining etiquette

In Vietnam, proper dining etiquette is a significant part of the culture; thus, it is essential for tourists to get familiar with and respect the country's dining norms. Meals in Vietnam are almost often served in the form of a family gathering, with a number of different dishes being brought out all at once and being passed around the table. When it comes to eating in Vietnam, here are some things to bear in mind:

- Wait to be seated: It is common practice to wait to be seated rather than seating yourself. The host or hostess will guide you to your seat.
- Chopsticks: Chopsticks are commonly used in Vietnam, and it is important to use them properly. Do not stick them into your rice bowl, as this is considered bad luck.
- Sharing food: As mentioned earlier, Vietnamese meals are typically served family-style, so it is common to share dishes with your dining companions. Do not take more than your share, and always use the serving utensils provided to take food from the shared dishes.
- Eating with your hands: It is acceptable to eat with your hands in Vietnam, but only for certain dishes, such as banh xeo, a type of Vietnamese pancake.
- Tipping: Tipping is not expected in Vietnam, but it is appreciated for exceptional service.

I remember a time when I was dining at a small, family-owned restaurant in Hanoi. I was served a bowl of soup and started blowing on it to cool it down. One of the restaurant owners gently told me that in Vietnam, it is considered impolite to blow on your food, as it is believed to be disrespectful to the chef. I thanked her for letting me know and made sure to eat my soup without blowing on it. It was a small mistake, but one that could have easily been avoided had I been aware of the local dining etiquette.

Chapter 8: Safety and Health

Safety tips for tourists

As with any travel destination, it is important to be aware of safety concerns when visiting Vietnam. Here are some tips to ensure a safe and enjoyable trip:

- Be aware of your surroundings and avoid walking alone at night, especially in unfamiliar areas. Stick to well-lit and crowded areas and consider using transportation services such as taxis or ride-sharing apps.
- Keep your valuables out of sight and secure. Pickpocketing can be an issue in crowded areas, so it's important to keep your belongings close to you and be mindful of your surroundings.
- Use common sense when it comes to food and drink. While Vietnamese cuisine is delicious, it's important to ensure that the food and water you consume is safe. Stick to bottled water and avoid eating food from street vendors that looks undercooked or has been sitting out for a long time.

- Be cautious when using public transportation. While trains and buses are generally safe, it's important to keep your belongings close to you and be aware of your surroundings when using these modes of transportation.
- Be mindful of traffic when crossing the street. Traffic in Vietnam can be chaotic, and it's important to exercise caution when crossing the street. Look both ways and walk at a steady pace when crossing and avoid stopping or changing direction suddenly.

Common scams to watch out for

Unfortunately, like many tourist destinations, there are some scams to be aware of in Vietnam. Here are some common ones to watch out for:

- The fake tour guide: Someone may approach you claiming to be a tour guide, but they are not licensed and may take you to overpriced shops or restaurants where they receive a commission. Always make sure to book tours and guides through a reputable company.
- The motorbike scam: Someone may offer you a ride on their motorbike, only to charge

you an exorbitant amount at the end of the ride. Always negotiate the price beforehand and make sure to agree on a price before getting on the bike.

- The fake currency scam: Be aware of counterfeit currency, especially the 500,000 VND note. Always check the notes carefully and make sure they are genuine before accepting them.
- The distraction scam: Someone may distract you by spilling something on you or creating a commotion while their accomplice steals your belongings. Always be aware of your surroundings and keep your belongings close to you.

To avoid these scams, always be aware of your surroundings and use common sense. Don't trust strangers too easily and always verify prices before agreeing to anything. It's also a good idea to research common scams before your trip so you can be prepared.

Health concerns and vaccinations

When traveling to Vietnam, it's important to take some health precautions to avoid getting sick. Here are some health concerns and recommended vaccinations to consider:

- Mosquito-borne diseases: Mosquitoes are prevalent in Vietnam and can spread diseases such as dengue fever, malaria, and Zika virus. Use insect repellent, wear long-sleeved clothing, and stay in air-conditioned or screened-in areas when possible.
- Food and water-borne illnesses: Travelers' diarrhea is a common ailment in Vietnam, often caused by consuming contaminated food or water. To avoid getting sick, stick to bottled water, avoid ice in drinks, and be careful with street food. Always wash your hands before eating.
- Air pollution: Some cities in Vietnam, particularly Hanoi and Ho Chi Minh City, have high levels of air pollution. If you have respiratory problems, it may be best to avoid these areas or wear a face mask.

Remember to carry any essential prescription drugs with you, since there is a possibility that they will either not be accessible in Vietnam or will be sold under a different brand name there. Always be prepared for the unexpected by carrying travel insurance and familiarizing yourself with the local medical facilities.

Chapter 9: Useful Phrases

Basic Vietnamese phrases for travelers

Here are some basic Vietnamese phrases for travelers:

- Hello - Xin chào (sin chow)
- Thank you - Cảm ơn (kahm uhn)
- Goodbye - Tạm biệt (tahm byeht)
- Yes - Vâng (vahng)
- No - Không (kohng)
- Please - Làm ơn (lam uhn)
- Sorry - Xin lỗi (sin loy)
- Excuse me - Xin lỗi (sin loy)
- I don't understand - Tôi không hiểu (toy kohng hyuh)
- Do you speak English? - Bạn có nói tiếng Anh không? (bahn koh noy teeeng ang kohng?)
- How much does this cost? - Cái này bao nhiêu tiền? (kai nay bao nyuh tee-en?)
- Where is the bathroom? - Nhà vệ sinh ở đâu? (nya vay sin uh dow?)
- Can you help me? - Bạn có thể giúp tôi được không? (bahn koh teu joop toy duoc kohng?)

- I need a doctor - Tôi cần một bác sĩ (toy cahn mot bahk si)
- Help! - Cứu tôi! (kyoo toy!)

Learning a few basic phrases can be helpful for communicating with locals and making your trip more enjoyable.

Numbers, time, and dates

here are some basic Vietnamese phrases for numbers, time, and dates:

Numbers:

- Zero: Không
- One: Một
- Two: Hai
- Three: Ba
- Four: Bốn
- Five: Năm
- Six: Sáu
- Seven: Bảy
- Eight: Tám
- Nine: Chín
- Ten: Mười

Time:

- What time is it? Mấy giờ rồi?
- It's [time]: [Time] giờ.
- Morning: Sáng
- Afternoon: Chiều
- Evening/Night: Tối

Dates:

- Today: Hôm nay
- Tomorrow: Ngày mai
- Yesterday: Hôm qua
- Day: Ngày
- Month: Tháng
- Year: Năm

I hope these phrases are helpful for your travels in Vietnam!

Emergencies

In case of an emergency while traveling in Vietnam, it's important to know how to ask for help and get assistance as quickly as possible. Here are some key phrases to keep in mind:

- Help! - Cứu với! (K-yoo voy)
- Police - Cảnh sát (K-ang saht)

- Hospital - Bệnh viện (Benh vee-en)
- Ambulance - Xe cứu thương (S-eh k-yoo toong)
- Fire - Lửa, cháy (L-oo-ah, chai)
- I need a doctor - Tôi cần một bác sĩ (Toy kun mot bahk see)
- Where is the hospital? - Bệnh viện ở đâu? (Benh vee-en uh dow?)
- Call an ambulance - Gọi xe cứu thương (G-oy se k-yoo toong)
- I have an emergency - Tôi có một trường hợp khẩn cấp (Toy koh mot chroong h-ohp kun cap)
- My friend needs help - Bạn tôi cần được giúp đỡ (Bun toy kun do-ook zoop duhp)

It's also a good idea to have the phone number for your embassy or consulate on hand in case of more serious emergencies. Make sure to keep important information like your passport, travel insurance, and emergency contacts in a safe and accessible place.

Chapter 10: Trade and Exports

Overview of Vietnam's economy and trade

During the course of the last several decades, the economy of Vietnam has maintained a status as one of those with the highest rates of growth anywhere in the globe. The nation's gross domestic product has increased at a steady pace of about 6-7% on a yearly basis, on average, and has even surpassed 7% in certain years since the country began participating in the global economy in the 1990s. In 2020, despite the effects of the COVID-19 pandemic, Vietnam's economy nevertheless increased by 2.91%, making it one of the few nations to sustain positive growth. This was despite the fact that Vietnam was one of the few countries to retain positive growth.

From the 1980s, the nation has moved away from a centrally planned economy and toward one that is geared more toward the market. Several substantial economic changes have occurred since the 1980s. The government has made measures to decrease obstacles to trade and investment, privatize state-owned firms, and promote foreign investment.

These moves were implemented in conjunction with other initiatives. As a consequence of this, Vietnam has transformed into a desirable location for international investors and is currently regarded as having one of the most open economies in the Southeast Asian region.

The textiles and garments, footwear, electrical goods, and agricultural sectors are the primary contributors to Vietnam's economy, which is highly reliant on exports. The country has emerged as a major node in global supply chains as a result of the large number of multinational corporations that have established manufacturing facilities there in order to take advantage of the country's inexpensive labor and advantageous economic climate. Also, Vietnam has signed a number of free trade agreements, one of which is with the European Union as well as the Comprehensive and Progressive Agreement for Trans-Pacific Partnership (CPTPP), both of which have further opened up access to markets all over the globe.

In recent years, Vietnam has been working toward the realization of a visionary plan to turn itself into a digital economy. The country's ultimate goal is to establish itself as a technological and innovative frontrunner in the region. The expansion of the information technology sector has been given high priority by the government, which has also supported the expansion of tech-related startups as well as small and medium-sized businesses (SMEs). This has resulted in the development of a thriving startup ecosystem in locations like as Ho Chi Minh City and Hanoi, where a large number of young entrepreneurs are initiating new businesses and drawing funding from a variety of domestic and international sources.

In spite of Vietnam's economic achievements, the country is nevertheless confronted with a variety of difficulties. There is a significant problem with income disparity, as shown by the fact that a large number of individuals in rural regions and ethnic minority groups are still living in poverty. Also, the nation struggles with environmental issues such as pollution in the air and water, loss of forest cover, and excessive fishing. In addition, investors and residents alike continue to have substantial worries over the prevalence of unethical practices and a lack of openness in both government and industry.

In the realm of international commerce, Vietnam has been making concerted efforts to broaden its export markets to include countries other than its traditional trading partners, such as the United States and the European Union. The nation has been investigating potential in Africa and the Middle

East, while at the same time strengthening its economic relations with other Asian nations, notably China, Japan, and South Korea. Moreover, Vietnam has been working toward achieving a higher level of regional integration via the implementation of programs such as the ASEAN Economic Community and the Regional Comprehensive Economic Partnership (RCEP), which brings together nations from all around Asia and Oceania.

In general, Vietnam's economy and commerce have gone through substantial changes over the last several decades, and the nation is now in a strong position to continue its growth and development in the years to come.

Major industries and products

The production of goods, the cultivation of crops, and the supply of services are some of Vietnam's key economic pillars. The economy of Vietnam is rather diversified. The country has had significant growth in these industries over the course of the last several decades, and as a direct consequence, it has emerged as a significant player in the economy of the whole globe.

Since it is one of Vietnam's most significant and largest sectors, the manufacturing sector is one of the most essential contributors to economic growth in the nation. The country has become a preferred place for the manufacturing sector as a consequence of its attractive investment regulations, competitive labor rates, and convenient location. As a result, the country has emerged as a preferred destination. The term "manufacturing" refers to an industry that encompasses a wide variety of sub-industries, some of which include automotive, textiles, footwear, food & drinks, and electronics. Other examples of sub-industries that fall under the umbrella of "manufacturing" include the beverage and food industries.

Agriculture is not only a significant contributor to Vietnam's gross domestic product but also one of the country's most important sectors in terms of the number of people it employs. Rice is the primary source of sustenance for the people of Vietnam, and this country is well-known across the world for its production of rice. Further examples of agricultural commodities are coffee, rubber, tea, cashews, and things generated from fisheries. Other examples of agricultural goods include cashews.

The fast growth of Vietnam's service sector in the economy may be attributed, in part, to the country's growing middle class as well as the country's burgeoning tourism industry. The phrase "services sector" refers to a broad economic category that incorporates a wide range of distinct industries, including retail, real estate, tourism, and financial services, amongst others.

In addition to these many kinds of enterprises, Vietnam is also a large producer and exporter of oil and gas, which together make up a considerable amount of the country's total economic production and are an essential source of revenue. The country has significant oil reserves, and it has made significant investments in the oil and gas sector of its economy in order to further harness its natural resources.

Popular export items and markets

Exporting accounts for a substantial portion of Vietnam's economy, and the nation is famous for a diverse range of goods, such as electronics, textiles, footwear, furniture, agricultural products, and seafood. The United States of America, Japan, China, and South Korea are some of the most significant markets for the country's exports.

Electronics: Vietnam has emerged as a major player in the global electronics industry, with a significant share in the production of smartphones, laptops, and other electronic components. This is due in large part to the country's low labor costs, which have allowed the country to attract foreign direct investment. This is due, in large part, to the cheap cost of labor in the nation, which has made it possible for the country to attract direct investment from other countries. Firms in the electronics business that are among the most well-known and influential include Samsung Electronics, LG Electronics, and Foxconn, among others.

Textiles and footwear: Vietnam is also a big exporter of textiles and footwear, and companies such as Nike, Adidas, and Gap get their goods from the country. The textile and footwear industries of Vietnam employ a considerable proportion of the country's labor force and are responsible for the employment of millions of people.

Vietnam is not only a key manufacturer of furniture but also a significant exporter of the goods, with companies such as Ikea acquiring it from the country. Because of the country's relatively low labor costs and abundant supply of wood, it has emerged as a formidable competitor in the worldwide furniture market.

Rice, along with coffee, cashew nuts, and black pepper, is considered to be one of the most significant agricultural commodities coming out of Vietnam. Rice is another agricultural product that Vietnam is a big exporter of across the globe. The country is a great place for agricultural initiatives to be carried out due to the moderate climate and the rich soil that it has.

Another big contributor to Vietnam's economy is the seafood sector, particularly shrimp and catfish, both of which are exported in substantial quantities from the nation. There are several opportunities for aquaculture in this nation as a result of the country's huge coastline, enormous network of rivers and canals, and quantity of waterways.

In recent years, Vietnam has placed a significant emphasis on growing its high-tech sectors, such as software development and renewable energy, in order to diversify its economy and reduce its reliance on businesses that are more historically significant. This is part of Vietnam's larger effort to reduce its economic dependence on businesses that are more globally significant.

Chapter 11: Recommended Tours and Itineraries

One-week itinerary

Here is a recommended one-week itinerary for Vietnam:

Day 1: Arrival in Hanoi

- Explore the Old Quarter of Hanoi, including Hoan Kiem Lake and the Temple of Literature.
- Attend a traditional water puppet show in the evening.

Day 2: Hanoi

- Visit the Ho Chi Minh Mausoleum and the One Pillar Pagoda.
- Explore the Hoa Lo Prison Museum.

Day 3: Halong Bay

- Take a day trip to Halong Bay and go on a boat cruise to see the stunning scenery.
- Try some fresh seafood for lunch on the boat.

Day 4: Hoi An

- Take a morning flight to Hoi An.
- Explore the charming Old Town and visit the Japanese Covered Bridge and the Assembly Hall of the Fujian Chinese Congregation.

Day 5: Hoi An

- Take a bicycle tour to the countryside and visit a local farm and fishing village.
- Take a cooking class to learn how to make some traditional Vietnamese dishes.

Day 6: Ho Chi Minh City

- Take a flight to Ho Chi Minh City.
- Visit the War Remnants Museum and the Reunification Palace.

Day 7: Ho Chi Minh City

- Explore the vibrant Ben Thanh Market and do some shopping for souvenirs.
- Take a trip to the Cu Chi Tunnels, an extensive network of underground tunnels used during the Vietnam War.

These itinerary covers some of the most popular destinations in Vietnam and offers a mix of cultural experiences, natural beauty, and historical landmarks. However, keep in mind that Vietnam is a large country with many attractions, so consider extending your trip if you have more time available.

Two-week itinerary

If you have two weeks to spend in Vietnam, you can explore more of the country and visit some of its most popular destinations. Here's a recommended two-week itinerary:

Day 1-3: Hanoi

- Explore the Old Quarter, Hoan Kiem Lake, and the Temple of Literature.
- Visit the Ho Chi Minh Mausoleum and Museum, One Pillar Pagoda, and the Presidential Palace.
- Watch a water puppet show and enjoy street food!

Day 4-6: Halong Bay

- Take a cruise in Halong Bay and visit the caves.
- Kayak and swim in the bay.
- Enjoy the sunset and sunrise on the boat.

Day 7-8: Ninh Binh

- Visit Tam Coc, also known as "Halong Bay on Land".
- Explore the Trang An Scenic Landscape Complex.
- Go biking or hiking in the countryside.

Day 9-11: Hoi An

- Wander around the ancient town of Hoi An.
- Take a cooking class and learn to make local dishes.
- Visit the My Son Sanctuary and the Cham Islands.

Day 12-13: Hue

- Explore the Imperial City and the Royal Tombs.
- Take a dragon boat tour on the Perfume River.
- Enjoy Hue's famous cuisine.

Day 14-15: Ho Chi Minh City

- Visit the War Remnants Museum and the Cu Chi Tunnels.
- Explore the city's colonial architecture.
- Enjoy street food and nightlife in District 1.

This itinerary covers the highlights of Vietnam, from the bustling capital of Hanoi to the stunning scenery of Halong Bay, the ancient town of Hoi An, and the historical city of Hue. You'll also get to experience the vibrant culture and delicious cuisine of the country. Keep in mind that there's so much more to explore in Vietnam, so feel free to adjust this itinerary to fit your interests and preferences.

Customizable tours

Customizable tours in Vietnam are a popular option for travelers who want to create a unique and personalized travel experience. These tours are often tailored to meet the specific interests and preferences of individual travelers, and can include a variety of activities, accommodations, and destinations.

Some popular customizable tour options in Vietnam include:

- Food and culinary tours - These tours allow travelers to explore the diverse and delicious cuisine of Vietnam, from street food to fine dining experiences.
- Cultural and historical tours - These tours focus on the rich history and traditions of Vietnam, taking travelers to important

cultural and historical sites such as temples, museums, and ancient cities.

- Adventure tours - These tours are designed for travelers who want to get off the beaten path and explore the natural beauty of Vietnam through activities such as trekking, kayaking, and cycling.
- Beach and island tours - Vietnam is home to some of the most beautiful beaches and islands in Southeast Asia, and these tours allow travelers to relax and soak up the sun in paradise-like settings.

It is crucial to deal with a reputable and experienced tour operator when planning a vacation in Vietnam. This will ensure that you get assistance in developing a customized schedule that caters to your specific requirements and tastes. While planning a personalized trip, it is essential to take into account a number of different aspects, including travel preferences, available funds, and time limits.

In general, tourists are given the opportunity to create an adventure that is one of a kind and one that will stick with them forever when they book a customized trip in Vietnam.

Conclusion

As our discussion on Vietnam draws to a close, I feel compelled to mention that it is an intriguing nation with a long and eventful past, a vibrant culture, and stunning natural scenery. Every tourist will find that Vietnam has a lot to offer them, from the hustle and bustle of its metropolis to the peace and quiet of its rural areas. There is something for everyone in Vietnam, whether you want excitement, leisure, or absorption in the local culture.

Throughout the course of our conversation, we spoke about a broad variety of subjects, such as the food, attractions, and traditions of the nation, among other things. We spoke about the greatest locations to visit, where to locate the finest street food, how to successfully navigate the culture of bargaining, and a lot of other things. In addition to this, we discussed the possible dangers to visitors' health as well as the safety problems they should be aware of.

Based on my own travels and experiences, I can confidently claim that Vietnam is a nation that is well worth visiting. My stay there was filled with wonderful experiences, such as discovering new towns and delectable cuisine, as well as gaining insight into the background and traditions of the nation. I can't stress enough how strongly I advise everyone to put a trip to Vietnam at the top of their travel bucket list and take advantage of all that this incredible nation has to offer.

Vietnam will not let you down, regardless of whether you go with one of our selected one- or two-week itineraries or design your own fully personalized journey around the country. Hence, gather your belongings, get yourself ready for an exciting journey, and immerse yourself in the splendor of Vietnam.

Printed in Great Britain
by Amazon

34329727R00076